GW00646590

An Invitation to Conversion

Lent and Easter
with Pope Francis

*All booklets are published thanks to the
generous support of the members of the
Catholic Truth Society*

CATHOLIC TRUTH SOCIETY
PUBLISHERS TO THE HOLY SEE

Contents

All rights reserved. First published 2017 by The Incorporated Catholic Truth Society, 40-46 Harleyford Road London SE11 5AY Tel: 020 7640 0042 Fax: 020 7640 0046. This edition © 2017 The Incorporated Catholic Truth Society, text © 2016 Libreria Editrice Vaticana.

ISBN 978 1 78469 152 3

SEASON OF LENT

ASH WEDNESDAY

The Word of God, at the start of the Lenten journey, addresses two invitations to the Church and to each of us.

The first is that of St Paul: "be reconciled to God" (*2 Co* 5:20). It is not simply good fatherly advice, neither is it just a suggestion; it is a bona fide supplication on Christ's behalf: "We beseech you on behalf of Christ, be reconciled to God" (ibid.). Why does he make such a solemn and earnest appeal? Because Christ knows how fragile and sinful we are, he knows the weakness of our heart. He immediately sees it wounded by the evil we have committed. He knows how much we need forgiveness, he knows that it is important for us to feel loved in order to do good. We cannot do it alone: this is why the Apostle does not tell us to do something but to allow ourselves to be reconciled with God, to let him forgive us, with trust, because "God is greater than our hearts" (*1 Jn* 3:20). He conquers sin and lifts us out of misery, if we let him. It is up to us to acknowledge that we need mercy. This is the first step on the Christian path; it entails entering through the open door which is Christ, where he, the Saviour, awaits us and offers us a new and joyful life.

The door of the heart

There may be a few obstacles, which close the door of the heart. There is the temptation to lock the doors, or to live with our sin, minimising it, always justifying it, thinking we are no worse than others; this, however, is how the locks of the soul are closed and we remain shut inside, prisoners of evil. Another obstacle is the shame of opening the secret door of the heart. Shame, in reality, is a good symptom, because it shows that we want to break away from evil; however, it must never be transformed into apprehension or fear. There is a third pitfall, that of distancing ourselves from the door: it happens when we hide in our misery, when we ruminate constantly, connecting it to negative things, until sinking into the darkest repositories of the soul. Then we even become kindred with the sorrow that we do not want, we become discouraged and we are weaker in the face of temptations. This happens because we bide alone with ourselves, closing ourselves off and avoiding the light; while the Lord's grace alone frees us. Therefore let us be reconciled, let us listen to Jesus who says to those who are weary and oppressed: "Come to me" (*Mt* 11:28). Not to dwell within themselves, but to go to him! Comfort and peace are there.

There is a second invitation of God, who says, through the prophet Joel: "return to me with all your heart" (2:12). If we need to return it is because we have distanced ourselves. It is the mystery of sin: we have distanced ourselves from God, from others, from ourselves. It is not difficult to realise this: we all see how we struggle to truly trust in God, to entrust ourselves to him as Father, without fear; as it is challenging to love others, rather than thinking badly of them; how it costs us to do our true good, while we are attracted and seduced by so many material realities, which disappear and in the end leave us impoverished. Alongside this history of sin, Jesus inaugurated a history of salvation. The Gospel which opens Lent calls us to be protagonists, embracing three remedies, three medicines which heal us from sin (cf. *Mt* 6:1-6, 16-18).

Trust in the Lord

In the first place is prayer, an expression of openness and trust in the Lord: it is the personal encounter with him, which shortens the distances created by sin. Praying means saying: "I am not self-sufficient, I need You, You are my life and my salvation". In the second place is charity, in order to overcome our lack of involvement with regard to others. True love, in fact, is not an outward act, it is not giving something in a paternalistic way in order to assuage the conscience, but to accept those who are in need of our time, our friendship, our help. It means living to serve, overcoming the temptation to satisfy ourselves. In the third place is fasting, penance, in order to free ourselves from dependencies regarding what is passing, and to train ourselves to be more sensitive and merciful. It is an invitation to simplicity and to sharing: to take something from our table and from our assets in order to once again find the true benefit of freedom.

"Return to me" - says the Lord - "return with all your heart": not only with a few outward deeds, but from the depths of our selves. Indeed, Jesus calls us to live prayer, charity and penance with consistency and authenticity, overcoming hypocrisy. May Lent be a beneficial time to "prune" falseness, worldliness, indifference: so as not to think that everything is fine if I am fine; so as to understand that what counts is not approval, the search for success or consensus, but the cleansing of the heart and of life; so as to find again our Christian identity, namely, the love that serves, not the selfishness that serves us. Let us embark on the journey together, as Church, by receiving ashes - we too will become ashes - and keeping our gaze fixed on the crucifix. He, loving us, invites us to be reconciled with God and to return to him, in order to find ourselves again.[1]

First Sunday of Lent

Last Wednesday we began the liturgical season of Lent, during which the Church invites us to prepare ourselves to celebrate the great feast of Easter. This is a special time for recalling the gift of our baptism, when we became children of God. The Church invites us to renew the gift she has given us, not to let this gift lie dormant as if it were something from the past or locked away in a "memory chest". Lent is a good time to recover the joy and hope that make us feel like beloved sons and daughters of the Father. The Father who waits for us in order to cast off our garments of exhaustion, of apathy, of mistrust, and so clothe us with the dignity which only a true father or mother knows how to give their children, with the garments born of tenderness and love.

Our Father, he is the Father of a great family; he is our Father. He knows that he has a unique love, but he does not know how to bear or raise an "only child". He is the God of the home, of brotherhood, of bread broken and shared. He is the God who is "Our Father", not "my father" or "your stepfather".

God's dream makes its home and lives in each one of us so that at every Easter, in every Eucharist we celebrate, we may be the children of God. It is a dream which so many of our brothers and sisters have had through history. A dream witnessed to by the blood of so many martyrs, both from long ago and from now.

A time of conversion

Lent is a time of conversion, of daily experiencing in our lives how this dream is continually threatened by the father of lies - and we hear in the Gospel how he acted towards Jesus - by the one who tries to separate us, making a divided and confrontational family; a society which is divided and at loggerheads, a society of the few, and for the few. How often we experience in our own lives, or in our own families, among our friends or neighbours, the pain which arises when the dignity we carry within is not recognised. How many times have we had to cry and regret on realising that we have not acknowledged this dignity in others. How often - and it pains me to say it - have we been blind and impervious in failing to recognise our own and others' dignity.

Lent is a time for reconsidering our feelings, for letting our eyes be opened to the frequent injustices which stand in direct opposition to the dream and the plan of God. It is a time to unmask three great temptations that wear down and fracture the image which God wanted to form in us:

There are three temptations of Christ... three temptations for the Christian, which seek to destroy what we have been called to be; three temptations which try to corrode us and tear us down.

First, wealth: seizing hold of goods destined for all, and using them only for "my own people". That is, taking "bread" based on the toil of others, or even at the expense of their very lives. That wealth which tastes of pain, bitterness and suffering. That is the bread that a corrupt family or society gives its own children.

The second temptation, vanity: the pursuit of prestige based on continuous, relentless exclusion of those who "are not like me". The futile chasing of those five minutes of fame which do not forgive the "reputation" of others. "Making firewood from a felled tree" gradually gives way to the third temptation, the worst. It is that of pride, or rather, putting oneself on a higher level than one truly is on, feeling that one does not share the life of "mere mortals", and yet being one who prays every day: "I thank you Lord that you have not made me like those others...".

The three temptations of Christ... Three temptations which the Christian is faced with daily. Three temptations which seek to corrode, destroy and extinguish the joy and freshness of the Gospel. Three temptations which lock us into a cycle of destruction and sin.

Choose Christ

It is worth asking ourselves:

To what degree are we aware of these temptations in our lives, in our very selves?

How much have we become accustomed to a lifestyle where we think that our source and life force lies only in wealth?

To what point do we feel that caring about others, our concern and work for bread, for the good name and dignity of others, are wellsprings of happiness and hope?

We have chosen Jesus, not the evil one. If we remember what we heard in the Gospel, Jesus does not reply to the devil with any of his own words, but rather he responds with the words of God, the words of scripture. Because brothers and sisters, and let us be clear about this, we cannot dialogue with the devil, we cannot do this because he will always win. Only the power of God's word can overcome him. We have opted for Jesus and not for the devil; we want to follow in Jesus's footsteps, even though we know that this is not easy. We know what it means to be seduced by money, fame and power. For this reason, the Church gives us the gift of this Lenten season, invites us to conversion, offering but one certainty: he is waiting for us and wants to heal our hearts of all that tears us down. He is the God who has a name: Mercy. His name is our wealth, his name is what makes us famous, his name is our power and in his name we say once more with the Psalm: "You are my God and in you I trust". Will you repeat it together? Three times: "You are my God and in you I trust". "You are my God and in you I trust".

In this Eucharist, may the Holy Spirit renew in us the certainty that his name is Mercy, and may he let us experience each day that "the Gospel fills the hearts and lives of all who encounter Jesus...", knowing that "with Christ and in Christ joy is constantly born anew" (cf. *Evangelii Gaudium*, 1).[2]

SECOND SUNDAY OF LENT

"I desire mercy, and not sacrifice" (Mt 9:13).

Mary, the image of a Church which evangelises because she is evangelised

In the Bull of Indiction of the Extraordinary Jubilee of Mercy, I asked that "the season of Lent in this Jubilee Year be lived more intensely as a privileged moment to celebrate and experience God's mercy" (*Misericordiae Vultus*, 17). By calling for an attentive listening to the word of God and encouraging the initiative "24 Hours for the Lord", I sought to stress the primacy of prayerful listening to God's word, especially his prophetic word. The mercy of God is a proclamation made to the world, a proclamation which each Christian is called to experience at first hand. For this reason, during the season of Lent I will send out Missionaries of Mercy as a concrete sign to everyone of God's closeness and forgiveness.

After receiving the Good News told to her by the Archangel Gabriel, Mary, in her *Magnificat*, prophetically sings of the mercy whereby God chose her. The Virgin of Nazareth, betrothed to Joseph, thus becomes the perfect icon of the Church which evangelises, for she was, and continues to be, evangelised by the Holy Spirit, who made her virginal womb fruitful. In the prophetic tradition, mercy is strictly related - even on the etymological level - to the maternal womb (*rahamim*) and to a generous, faithful and compassionate goodness (*hesed*) shown within marriage and family relationships.

God's covenant with humanity: a history of mercy

The mystery of divine mercy is revealed in the history of the covenant between God and his people Israel. God shows himself ever rich in mercy, ever ready to treat his people with deep tenderness and compassion, especially at those tragic moments when infidelity ruptures the bond of the covenant, which then needs to be ratified more firmly in justice and truth. Here is a true love story, in which God plays the role of the betrayed father and husband, while Israel plays the unfaithful child and bride. These domestic images - as in the case of Hosea (cf. *Ho* 1-2) - show to what extent God wishes to bind himself to his people.

This love story culminates in the incarnation of God's Son. In Christ, the Father pours forth his boundless mercy even to making him "mercy incarnate" (*Misericordiae Vultus*, 8). As a man, Jesus of Nazareth is a true son of Israel; he embodies that perfect hearing required of every Jew by the *Shema*, which today too is the heart of God's covenant with Israel: "Hear, O Israel: The Lord our God is one Lord; and you shall love the Lord your God with all your heart, and with all your soul, and with all your might" (*Dt* 6:4-5). As the Son of God, he is the Bridegroom who does everything to win over the love of his bride, to whom he is bound by an unconditional love which becomes visible in the eternal wedding feast.

This is the very heart of the apostolic *kerygma*, in which divine mercy holds a central and fundamental place. It is "the beauty of the saving love of God made manifest in Jesus Christ who died and rose from the dead" (*Evangelii Gaudium*, 36), that first proclamation which "we must hear again and again in different ways, the one which we must announce one way or another throughout the process of catechesis, at every level and moment" (ibid., 164). Mercy "expresses God's way of reaching out to the sinner, offering him a new chance to look at himself, convert, and believe" (*Misericordiae Vultus*, 21), thus restoring his relationship with him. In Jesus crucified, God shows his desire to draw near to sinners, however far they may have strayed from him. In this way he hopes to soften the hardened heart of his Bride.

The works of mercy

God's mercy transforms human hearts; it enables us, through the experience of a faithful love, to become merciful in turn. In an ever new miracle, divine mercy shines forth in our lives, inspiring each of us to love our neighbour and to devote ourselves to what the Church's tradition calls the spiritual and corporal works of mercy. These works remind us that faith finds expression in concrete everyday actions meant to help our neighbours in body and spirit: by feeding, visiting, comforting and instructing them. On such things will we be judged. For this reason, I expressed my hope that "the Christian people may reflect on the corporal and spiritual works of mercy; this will be a way to reawaken our conscience, too often grown dull in the face of poverty, and to enter more deeply into the heart of the Gospel where the poor have a special experience of God's mercy" (ibid., 15). For in the poor, the flesh of Christ "becomes visible in the flesh of the tortured, the crushed, the scourged, the malnourished, and the exiled… to be acknowledged, touched, and cared for by us" (ibid.). It is the unprecedented and scandalous mystery of the extension in time of the suffering of the Innocent Lamb, the burning bush of gratuitous love. Before this love, we can, like Moses, take off our sandals (cf. *Ex* 3:5), especially when the poor are our brothers or sisters in Christ who are suffering for their faith.

Love as strong as death

In the light of this love, which is strong as death (cf. *Song* 8:6), the real poor are revealed as those who refuse to see themselves as such. They consider themselves rich, but they are actually the poorest of the poor. This is because they are slaves to sin, which leads them to use wealth and power not for the service of God and others, but to stifle within their hearts the profound sense that they too are only poor beggars. The greater their power and wealth, the more this blindness and deception can grow. It can even reach the point of being blind to Lazarus begging at their doorstep (cf. *Lk* 16:20-21). Lazarus, the poor man, is a figure of Christ, who through the poor pleads for our conversion. As such, he represents the possibility of conversion which God offers us and which we may well fail to see. Such blindness is often accompanied by the proud illusion of our own omnipotence, which reflects in a sinister way the diabolical "you will be like God" (*Gn* 3:5) which is the root of all sin. This illusion can likewise take social and political forms, as shown by the totalitarian systems of the twentieth century, and, in our own day, by the ideologies of monopolising thought and technoscience, which would make God irrelevant and reduce man to raw material to be exploited. This illusion can also be seen in the sinful structures linked to a model of false development based on the idolatry of money, which leads to lack of concern for the fate of the poor on the part of wealthier individuals and societies; they close their doors, refusing even to see the poor.

Love alone is the answer

For all of us, then, the season of Lent in this Jubilee Year is a favourable time to overcome our existential alienation by listening to God's word and by practising the works of mercy. In the corporal works of mercy we touch the flesh of Christ in our brothers and sisters who need to be fed, clothed, sheltered, visited; in the spiritual works of mercy - counsel, instruction, forgiveness, admonishment and prayer - we touch more directly our own sinfulness. The corporal and spiritual works of mercy must never be separated. By touching the flesh of the crucified Jesus in the suffering, sinners can receive the gift of realising that they too are poor and in need. By taking this path, the "proud", the "powerful" and the "wealthy" spoken of in the *Magnificat* can also be embraced and undeservedly loved by the crucified Lord who died and rose for them. This love alone is the answer to that yearning for infinite happiness and love that we think we can satisfy with the idols of knowledge, power and riches. Yet the danger always remains that by a constant refusal to open the doors of their hearts to Christ who knocks on them in the poor, the proud, rich and powerful will end up condemning themselves and plunging into the eternal abyss of solitude which is hell. The pointed words of Abraham apply to them and to all of us: "They have Moses and the prophets; let them hear them" (*Lk* 16:29). Such attentive listening will best prepare us to celebrate the final victory over sin and death of the Bridegroom, now risen, who desires to purify his Betrothed in expectation of his coming.

Let us not waste this season of Lent, so favourable a time for conversion! We ask this through the maternal intercession of the Virgin Mary, who, encountering the greatness of God's mercy freely bestowed upon her, was the first to acknowledge her lowliness (cf. *Lk* 1:48) and to call herself the Lord's humble servant (cf. *Lk* 1:38).[3]

THIRD SUNDAY OF LENT

In today's Gospel passage, Jesus refers to two tragic events which had caused a stir: a cruel suppression carried out by Roman soldiers in the Temple, and the collapse of the tower of Siloam in Jerusalem, which resulted in eighteen deaths (cf. *Lk* 13:1-5).

Jesus is aware of the superstitious mentality of his listeners and he knows that they misinterpreted that type of event. In fact, they thought that, if those people died in such a cruel way it was a sign that God was punishing them for some grave sin they had committed, as if to say "they deserved it". Instead, the fact that they were saved from such a disgrace made them feel "good about themselves". They "deserved it"; "I'm fine".

Jesus clearly rejects this outlook, because God does not allow tragedies in order to punish sins, and he affirms that those poor victims were no worse than others. Instead, he invites his listeners to draw from these sad events a lesson that applies to everyone, because we are all sinners; in fact, he said to those who questioned him, "Unless you repent you will all likewise perish" (v. 3).

Today too, seeing certain misfortunes and sorrowful events, we can be tempted to "unload" the responsibility onto the victims, or even onto God himself. But the Gospel invites us to reflect: what idea do we have of God? Are we truly convinced that God is like that, or isn't that just our projection, a god made to "our image and likeness"?

Take up the path of the Gospel

Jesus, on the contrary, invites us to change our heart, to make a radical about-face on the path of our lives, to abandon compromises with evil - and this is something we all do, compromises with evil, hypocrisy... I think that nearly all of us has a little hypocrisy - in order to decidedly take up the path of the Gospel. But again there is the temptation to justify ourselves. What should we convert from? Aren't we basically good people? How many times have we thought this: "But after all I am a good man, I'm a good woman"... isn't that true? "Am I not a believer and even quite a churchgoer?" And we believe that this way we are justified.

Unfortunately, each of us strongly resembles the tree that, over many years, has repeatedly shown that it's infertile. But, fortunately for us, Jesus is like a farmer who, with limitless patience, still obtains a concession for the fruitless vine. "Let it alone this year" - he said to the owner - "we shall see if it bears fruit next year" (cf. v. 9).

A "year" of grace: the period of Christ's ministry, the time of the Church before his glorious return, an interval of our life, marked by a certain number of Lenten seasons, which are offered to us as occasions of repentance and salvation, the duration of a Jubilee Year of Mercy. The invincible patience of Jesus! Have you thought about the patience of God? Have you ever thought as well of his limitless concern for sinners? How it should lead us to impatience with ourselves! It's never too late to convert, never. God's patience awaits us until the last moment.

The patience of God

Remember that little story from St Thérèse of the Child Jesus, when she prayed for that man who was condemned to death, a criminal, who did not want to receive the comfort of the Church. He rejected the priest, he didn't want [forgiveness], he wanted to die like that. And she prayed in the convent, and when, at the moment of being executed, the man turned to the priest, took the crucifix and kissed it. The patience of God! He does the same with us, with all of us. How many times, we don't know - we'll know in heaven - but how many times we are there, there... [about to fall off the edge] and the Lord saves us. He saves us because he has great patience with us. And this is his mercy. It's never too late to convert, but it's urgent. Now is the time! Let us begin today.

May the Virgin Mary sustain us, so that we can open our hearts to the grace of God, to his mercy; and may she help us to never judge others, but rather to allow ourselves to be struck by daily misfortunes and to make a serious examination of our consciences and to repent.[4]

FOURTH SUNDAY OF LENT

In Chapter 15 of Luke's Gospel, we find three parables of mercy: that of the sheep found (vv. 4-7), that of the coin found (vv. 8-10), and the great parable of the prodigal son, or rather, of the merciful father (vv. 11-32). Today, it would be nice for each of us to open Chapter 15 of the Gospel according to Luke, and read these three parables. During the Lenten itinerary, the Gospel presents to us this very parable of the merciful Father, featuring a father with his two sons. The story highlights some features of this father who is a man always ready to forgive and to hope against hope. Especially striking is the father's tolerance before the younger son's decision to leave home: he could have opposed it, knowing that he was still immature, a youth, or sought a lawyer not to give him his inheritance, as the father was still living. Instead, he allows the son to leave, although foreseeing the possible risks. God works with us like this: he allows us to be free, even to making mistakes, because in creating us, he has given us the great gift of freedom. It is for us to put it to good use. This gift of freedom that God gives us always amazes me!

But the separation from his son is only physical; for the father always carries him in his heart; trustingly, he awaits his return; the father watches the road in the hope of seeing him. And one day he sees him appear in the distance (cf. v. 20). But this means that this father, every day, would climb up to the terrace to see if his son was coming back! Thus the father is moved to see him, he runs toward him, embraces him, kisses him. So much tenderness! And this son got into trouble! But the father still welcomes him so.

The father treated the eldest son the same way, but as he had always stayed at home, he is now indignant and complains because he does not understand and does not share all that kindness toward his brother that had wronged. The father also goes to meet this son and reminds him that they were always together, they share everything (v. 31), one must welcome with joy the brother who has finally returned home. And this makes me think of something: When one feels one is a sinner, one feels worthless, or as I've heard some - many - say: "Father, I am like dirt", so then, this is the moment to go to the Father. Instead, when one feels righteous - "I always did the right thing …" - equally, the Father comes to seek us, because this attitude of feeling "right", is the wrong attitude: it is pride! It comes from the devil. The Father waits for those who recognise they are sinners and goes in search of the ones who feel "righteous". This is our Father!

The Servant Son

In this parable, you can also glimpse a third son. A third son? Where? He's hidden! And it is the one, "who, though he was in the form of God, did not count equality with God a thing to be grasped, but emptied himself, taking the form of a servant" (*Ph* 2:6-7). This Servant-Son is Jesus!

He is the extension of the arms and heart of the Father: he welcomed the prodigal Son and washed his dirty feet; he prepared the banquet for the feast of forgiveness. He, Jesus, teaches us to be "merciful as the Father is merciful".

The figure of the Father in the parable reveals the heart of God. He is the Merciful Father who, in Jesus, loves us beyond measure, always awaits our conversion every time we make mistakes; he awaits our return when we turn away from him thinking, we can do without him; he is always ready to open his arms no matter what happened. As the father of the Gospel, God also continues to consider us his children, even when we get lost, and comes to us with tenderness when we return to him. He addresses us so kindly when we believe we are right. The errors we commit, even if bad, do not wear out the fidelity of his love. In the Sacrament of Reconciliation, we can always start out anew: He welcomes us, gives us the dignity of being his children and tells us: "Go ahead! Be at peace! Rise, go ahead!"

In this time of Lent that still separates us from Easter, we are called to intensify the inner journey of conversion. May the loving gaze of our Father touch us. Let us return and return to him with all our heart, rejecting any compromise with sin. May the Virgin Mary accompany us until the regenerating embrace with Divine Mercy.[5]

FIFTH SUNDAY OF LENT

The Gospel of this Fifth Sunday of Lent (cf. *Jn* 8:1-11) is so beautiful, I really enjoy reading and rereading it. It presents the episode of the adulterous woman, highlighting the theme of the mercy of God, who never wants the sinner to die, but that the sinner convert and live. The scene unfolds on the Temple grounds. Imagine that there on the parvis [of St Peter's Basilica], Jesus is teaching the people, when several scribes and Pharisees arrive, dragging before him a woman caught in adultery. That woman is thus placed between Jesus and the crowd (cf. v. 3), between the mercy of the Son of God and the violence and anger of her accusers. In fact, they did not come to the Teacher to ask his opinion - they were bad people - but to ensnare him. Indeed, were Jesus to follow the stringent law, approving that the woman be stoned, he would lose his reputation of meekness and goodness which so fascinated the people; however, were he to be merciful, he would be flouting the law, which he himself said he did not wish to abolish but fulfil (cf. *Mt* 5:17). This is the situation Jesus is placed in.

This wicked intention was hidden behind the question that they asked Jesus: "What do you say about her?" (*Jn* 8:5) Jesus did not respond; he kept silent and made a mysterious gesture: he "bent down and wrote with his finger on the ground" (v. 7). Perhaps he was drawing, some said that he wrote down the sins of the Pharisees... however, he was writing, as if he were elsewhere. In this way he helped everyone to calm down, not to act on the wave of impulsiveness, and to seek the justice of God. But those wicked men persisted and waited for him to answer. They seemed to thirst for blood. Then Jesus looked up and said: "Let him who is without sin among you be the first to throw a stone at her" (v. 7). This response confounded the accusers, disarming all of them in the true sense of the word: they all lay down their "weapons", that is, the stones ready to be thrown, both the visible ones against the woman and those concealed against Jesus. While the Lord continued to write on the ground, to draw, I don't know... The accusers went away, one after the other, heads down, beginning with the eldest, most aware of not being without sin. How much good it does us to be aware that we too are sinners! When we speak ill of others - something we know well - how much good it will do us to have the courage to drop down the stones we have to throw at others, and to think a little about our own sins!

His merciful gaze

Only the woman and Jesus remained: misery and mercy. How often does this happen to us when we stop before the confessional, with shame, to show our misery and ask for forgiveness! "Woman, where are they?" (v. 10), Jesus said to her. This question is enough, and his merciful gaze, full of love, in order to let that person feel - perhaps for the first time - that she has dignity, that she is not her sin, she has personal dignity; that she can change her life, she can emerge from her slavery and walk on a new path.

Dear brothers and sisters, that woman represents all of us. We are sinners, meaning adulterers before God, betrayers of his fidelity. Her experience represents God's will for each of us: not our condemnation but our salvation through Jesus. He is the grace which saves from sin and from death. On the ground, in the dust of which every human being is made (*Gn* 2:7), he wrote God's sentence: "I want not that you die but that you live". God does not nail us to our sin, he does not identify us by the evil we have committed. We have a name, and God does not identify this name with the sin we have committed. He wants to free us, and wants that we too want it together with him. He wants us to be free to convert from evil to good, and this is possible - it is possible! - with his grace.

May the Virgin Mary help us to entrust ourselves completely to God's mercy, in order to become new creatures.[6]

HOLY WEEK AND TRIDUUM

Palm Sunday

"Blessed is he who comes in the name of the Lord!" (cf. *Lk* 19:38), the crowd of Jerusalem exclaimed joyfully as they welcomed Jesus. We have made that enthusiasm our own: by waving our olive and palm branches we have expressed our praise and our joy, our desire to receive Jesus who comes to us. Just as he entered Jerusalem, so he desires to enter our cities and our lives. As he did in the Gospel, riding on a donkey, so too he comes to us in humility; he comes "in the name of the Lord". Through the power of his divine love he forgives our sins and reconciles us to the Father and with ourselves.

Jesus is pleased with the crowd's showing their affection for him. When the Pharisees ask him to silence the children and the others who are acclaiming him, he responds: "I tell you, if these were silent, the very stones would cry out" (*Lk* 19:40). Nothing could dampen their enthusiasm for Jesus's entry. May nothing prevent us from finding in him the source of our joy, true joy, which abides and brings peace; for it is Jesus alone who saves us from the snares of sin, death, fear and sadness.

Today's liturgy teaches us that the Lord has not saved us by his triumphal entry or by means of powerful miracles.

The Apostle Paul, in the second reading, epitomises in two verbs the path of redemption: Jesus "emptied" and "humbled" himself (*Ph* 2:7-8). These two verbs show the boundlessness of God's love for us. Jesus emptied himself: he did not cling to the glory that was his as the Son of God, but became the Son of man in order to be in solidarity with us sinners in all things; yet he was without sin. Even more, he lived among us in "the condition of a servant" (v. 7); not of a king or a prince, but of a servant. Therefore he humbled himself, and the abyss of his humiliation, as Holy Week shows us, seems to be bottomless.

True love consists in concrete service

The first sign of this love "without end" (*Jn* 13:1) is the washing of the feet. "The Lord and Master" (*Jn* 13:14) stoops to his disciples' feet, as only servants would have done. He shows us by example that we need to allow his love to reach us, a love which bends down to us; we cannot do any less, we cannot love without letting ourselves be loved by him first, without experiencing his surprising tenderness and without accepting that true love consists in concrete service.

But this is only the beginning. The humiliation of Jesus reaches its utmost in the Passion: he is sold for thirty pieces of silver and betrayed by the kiss of a disciple whom he had chosen and called his friend. Nearly all the others flee and abandon him; Peter denies him three times in the courtyard of the Temple. Humiliated in his spirit by mockery, insults and spitting, he suffers in his body terrible brutality: the blows, the scourging and the crown of thorns make his face unrecognisable. He also experiences shame and disgraceful condemnation by religious and political authorities: he is made into sin and considered to be unjust. Pilate then sends him to Herod, who in turn sends him to the Roman governor. Even as every form of justice is denied to him, Jesus also experiences in his own flesh indifference, since no one wishes to take responsibility for his fate. And I think of the many people, so many outcasts, so many asylum seekers, so many refugees, all of those for whose fate no one wishes to take responsibility. The crowd, who just a little earlier had acclaimed him, now changes their praise into a cry of accusation, even to the point of preferring that a murderer be released in his place. And so the hour of death on the cross arrives, that most painful form of shame reserved for traitors, slaves and the worst kind of criminals. But isolation, defamation and pain are not yet the full extent of his deprivation. To be totally in solidarity with us, he also experiences on the cross the mysterious abandonment of the Father. In his abandonment, however, he prays and entrusts himself: "Father, into your hands I commit my spirit" (*Lk* 23:46). Hanging from the wood of the cross, beside derision he now confronts the last temptation: to come down from the cross, to conquer evil by might and to show the face of a powerful and invincible God. Jesus, however, even here at the height of his annihilation, reveals the true face of God, which is mercy. He forgives those who are crucifying him, he opens the gates of paradise to the repentant thief and he touches the heart of the centurion. If the mystery of evil is unfathomable, then the reality of Love poured out through him is infinite, reaching even to the tomb and to hell. He takes upon himself all our pain that he may redeem it, bringing light to darkness, life to death, love to hatred.

God's way of acting may seem so far removed from our own, that he was annihilated for our sake, while it seems difficult for us to even forget ourselves a little. He comes to save us; we are called to choose his way: the way of service, of giving, of forgetfulness of ourselves. Let us walk this path, pausing in these days to gaze upon the crucifix; it is the "royal seat of God". I invite you during this week to gaze often upon this "royal seat of God", to learn about the humble love which saves and gives life, so that we may give up all selfishness, and the seeking of power and fame. By humbling himself, Jesus invites us to walk on his path. Let us turn our faces to him, let us ask for the grace to understand at least something of the mystery of his obliteration for our sake; and then, in silence, let us contemplate the mystery of this Week.[7]

Triduum

We will live Holy Thursday, Good Friday and Holy Saturday as powerful moments that allow us to enter ever further into the great mystery of our faith: the Resurrection of Our Lord Jesus Christ. Everything in these three days speaks of mercy, because it makes visible the extent of God's love. We will listen to the account of the final days of Jesus's life. John the Evangelist offers us the key to understanding its profound meaning: "having loved his own who were in the world, he loved them to the end" (*Jn* 13:1). The love of God has no bounds. As St Augustine often repeated, it is a love that goes "to the end without end". God truly offers all of himself for each of us and holds nothing back. The Mystery which we adore in this Holy Week is a great history of love which knows no obstacles. The Passion of Jesus lasts until the end of the world, because it is a story of sharing in the suffering of all humanity and a permanent presence in the events of the private life of each of us. Indeed, the Easter Triduum is the commemoration of a drama of love which gives us the certainty that we will never be abandoned in life's trials.

On Holy Thursday Jesus institutes the Eucharist, anticipating in the Passover banquet his sacrifice on

Golgotha. In order to make the Apostles understand the love which enlivens him he washes their feet, offering once again in the first person the example of how they must act. The Eucharist is the love that becomes service. It is the sublime presence of Christ who wishes to relieve from hunger every man and woman, especially the weakest, to enable them to undertake a journey of witnessing amid the difficulties of the world. Moreover, in giving himself to us as food, Jesus attests that we must learn to share this nourishment with others so that it may become a true communion of life with those who are in need. He gives himself to us and asks us to dwell in him in order to do likewise.

The culminating moment of love

Good Friday is the culminating moment of love. The death of Jesus, who on the cross surrenders himself to the Father in order to offer salvation to the entire world, expresses love given to the end, a love without end. A love that seeks to embrace everyone, that excludes no one. A love that extends over time and space: an inexhaustible source of salvation to which each of us, sinners, can draw. If God has shown us his supreme love in the death of Jesus, then we too, regenerated by the Holy Spirit, can and must love one another.

Lastly, Holy Saturday is the day of God's silence. It must be a day of silence, and we must do everything possible so that for us it may truly be a day of silence, as it was in that time: the day of the silence of God. Jesus laid in the sepulchre shares with all of humanity in the tragedy of death. It is a silence which speaks and expresses love as solidarity with those who have always been neglected, whom the Son of God reaches, filling the emptiness that only the infinite mercy of God the Father can fill.

God is silent, but out of love. On this day, love - that silent love - becomes the expectation of life in the resurrection. Let us think about Holy Saturday: it will do us good to consider the silence of Our Lady, "the Believer", who awaited the Resurrection in silence. Our Lady will be, for us, the icon of Holy Saturday. Think hard about how Our Lady lived that Holy Saturday; in expectation. It is love that has no doubt, but which hopes in the word of the Lord, that it may be made manifest and resplendent on the day of Easter.

"If I could suffer more, I would"

It is all a great mystery of love and mercy. Our words are poor and insufficient to express it fully. We may find helpful the experience of a young woman, not very well known, who wrote sublime pages about the love of Christ. Her name was Julian of Norwich. She was illiterate, this girl who had visions of the Passion of Jesus and who then, after becoming a recluse, described, with simple but deep and intense language, the meaning of merciful love. She said: "Then our good Lord asked me: 'Are you glad that I suffered for you?'. I answered him: 'Yes, good Lord, and I am most grateful to you; yes, good Lord, may You be blessed'. Then Jesus, our good Lord, said: 'If you are glad, so too am I. Having suffered the passion for you is for me joy, happiness, eternal bliss; and if I could suffer more I would'". This is our Jesus, who says to each of us: "If I could suffer more for you, I would".

How beautiful these words are! They allow us to truly understand the immense and boundless love that the Lord has for each one of us. Let us allow ourselves to be wrapped in this mercy which comes to meet us; and in these days, as we keep our gaze fixed on the Passion and death of the Lord, let us receive in our heart his boundless love and, like Our Lady on Saturday, in silence, await the Resurrection.[8]

MAUNDY THURSDAY

Actions speak louder than images and words. Acts... There are, in this Word of God that we have read, two acts: Jesus who serves, who washes feet... He, who was the "master", washes the feet of others, his [disciples], of the least. An act. The second act: Judas who goes to Jesus's enemies, to those who do not want peace with Jesus, in order to take the money for which he betrayed him, thirty pieces of silver. Two acts. Today too, here, there are two acts: this one, all of us, together: Muslims, Hindus, Catholics, Copts, Evangelicals, but brothers and sisters, children of the same God, who want to live in peace, integrated. An act. Three days ago, an act of war, of destruction in a European city, by people who do not want to live in peace. But behind that act, as behind Judas, there were others. Behind Judas were those who paid money for Jesus to be delivered. Behind "that" act [in Brussels] are weapons producers and traffickers who want blood, not peace; who want war, not brotherhood.

Two parallel acts: on the one hand, Jesus washes the feet, while Judas sells Jesus for money; and on the other hand, you, we, everyone together, different religions, different cultures, but children of the same Father, brothers and sisters, while those unfortunate ones buy weapons to destroy brotherhood. Today, at this moment, as I perform the same act as Jesus by washing the feet of you twelve, we are all engaged in the act of brotherhood, and we are all saying: "We are diverse, we are different, we have different cultures and religions, but we are brothers and sisters and we want to live in peace". This is the act that I carry out with you. Each of us has a history on our shoulders, each of you has a history on your shoulders: so many crosses, so much pain, but also an open heart that wants brotherhood. Each one, in your own religious language, pray the Lord that this brotherhood infect the world, that there be no thirty pieces of silver to kill a brother, that there always be brotherhood and goodness. Let it be.[9]

HOLY SATURDAY

"Peter ran to the tomb" (*Lk* 24:12). What thoughts crossed Peter's mind and stirred his heart as he ran to the tomb? The Gospel tells us that the eleven, including Peter, had not believed the testimony of the women, their Easter proclamation. Quite the contrary, "these words seemed to them an idle tale" (v. 11). Thus there was doubt in Peter's heart, together with many other worries: sadness at the death of the beloved Master and disillusionment for having denied him three times during his Passion.

There is, however, something which signals a change in him: after listening to the women and refusing to believe them, "Peter rose" (v. 12). He did not remain sedentary, in thought; he did not stay at home as the others did. He did not succumb to the sombre atmosphere of those days, nor was he overwhelmed by his doubts. He was not consumed by remorse, fear or the continuous gossip that leads nowhere. He was looking for Jesus, not himself. He preferred the path of encounter and trust. And so, he got up, just as he was, and ran towards the tomb from where he would return "amazed" (v. 12). This marked the beginning of Peter's resurrection, the resurrection of his heart. Without giving in to sadness or darkness, he made room for hope: he allowed the light of God to enter into his heart, without smothering it.

The women too, who had gone out early in the morning to perform a work of mercy, taking the perfumed ointments to the tomb, had the same experience. They were "frightened and bowed their faces", and yet they were deeply affected by the words of the angel: "Why do you seek the living among the dead?" (v. 5)

We cannot discover life by being sad

We, like Peter and the women, cannot discover life by being sad, bereft of hope. Let us not stay imprisoned within ourselves, but let us break open our sealed tombs to the Lord - each of us knows what they are - so that he may enter and grant us life. Let us give him the stones of our rancour and the boulders of our past, those heavy burdens of our weaknesses and falls. Christ wants to come and take us by the hand to bring us out of our anguish. This is the first stone to be moved aside this night: the lack of hope which imprisons us within ourselves. May the Lord free us from this trap, from being Christians without hope, who live as if the Lord were not risen, as if our problems were the centre of our lives.

We see and will continue to see problems both within and without. They will always be there. But tonight it is important to shed the light of the Risen Lord upon our problems, and in a certain sense, to "evangelise" them.

To evangelise our problems. Let us not allow darkness and fear to distract us and control us; we must cry out to them: the Lord "is not here, but has risen!" (v. 6) He is our greatest joy; he is always at our side and will never let us down.

This is the foundation of our hope, which is not mere optimism, nor a psychological attitude or desire to be courageous. Christian hope is a gift that God gives us if we come out of ourselves and open our hearts to him. This hope does not disappoint us because the Holy Spirit has been poured into our hearts (cf. *Rm* 5:5). The Paraclete does not make everything look appealing. He does not remove evil with a magic wand. But he pours into us the vitality of life, which is not the absence of problems, but the certainty of being loved and always forgiven by Christ, who for us has conquered sin, conquered death and conquered fear. Today is the celebration of our hope, the celebration of this truth: nothing and no one will ever be able to separate us from his love (cf. *Rm* 8:39).

The Lord is alive

The Lord is alive and wants to be sought among the living. After having found him, each person is sent out by him to announce the Easter message, to awaken and resurrect hope in hearts burdened by sadness, in those who struggle to find meaning in life. This is so necessary today. However, we must not proclaim ourselves. Rather, as joyful servants of hope, we must announce the Risen One by our lives and by our love; otherwise we will be only an international organisation full of followers and good rules, yet incapable of offering the hope for which the world longs.

How can we strengthen our hope? The liturgy of this night offers some guidance. It teaches us to remember the works of God. The readings describe God's faithfulness, the history of his love towards us. The living word of God is able to involve us in this history of love, nourishing our hope and renewing our joy. The Gospel also reminds us of this: in order to kindle hope in the hearts of the women, the angel tells them: "Remember what [Jesus] told you" (v. 6). Remember the words of Jesus, remember all that he has done in our lives. Let us not forget his words and his works, otherwise we will lose hope and become "hopeless" Christians. Let us instead remember the Lord, his goodness and his life-giving words which have touched us. Let us remember them and make them ours, to be sentinels of the morning who know how to help others see the signs of the Risen Lord.

Dear brothers and sisters, Christ is risen! And we have the possibility of opening our hearts and receiving his gift of hope. Let us open our hearts to hope and go forth. May the memory of his works and his words be the bright star which directs our steps in the ways of faith towards that Easter that will have no end.[10]

EASTERTIDE

Easter Sunday

*"O give thanks to the Lord, for he is good,
for his mercy endures for ever"* (Ps 135:1)

Jesus Christ, the incarnation of God's mercy, out of love
for us, died on the cross, and out of love he rose again from
the dead. That is why we proclaim today: Jesus is Lord!

His Resurrection fulfils the prophecy of the Psalm:
God's mercy endures for ever; it never dies. We can trust
him completely, and we thank him because for our sake he
descended into the depths of the abyss.

Before the spiritual and moral abysses of mankind,
before the chasms that open up in hearts and provoke
hatred and death, only an infinite mercy can bring us
salvation. Only God can fill those chasms with his love,
prevent us from falling into them and help us to continue
our journey together towards the land of freedom and life.

The glorious Easter message, that Jesus, who was
crucified is not here but risen (cf. *Mt* 28:5-6), offers us
the comforting assurance that the abyss of death has been
bridged and, with it, all mourning, lamentation and pain
(cf. *Rv* 21:4). The Lord, who suffered abandonment by
his disciples, the burden of an unjust condemnation and
shame of an ignominious death, now makes us sharers

of his immortal life and enables us to see with his eyes of love and compassion those who hunger and thirst, strangers and prisoners, the marginalised and the outcast, the victims of oppression and violence. Our world is full of persons suffering in body and spirit, even as the daily news is full of stories of brutal crimes which often take place within homes, and large-scale armed conflicts which cause indescribable suffering to entire peoples.

The weapons of love

With the weapons of love, God has defeated selfishness and death. His son Jesus is the door of mercy wide open to all. May efforts be made everywhere to promote the culture of counter, justice and reciprocal respect, which alone can guarantee the spiritual and material welfare of all people.

The Easter message of the risen Christ, a message of life for all humanity, echoes down the ages and invites us not to forget those men and women seeking a better future, an ever more numerous throng of migrants and refugees - including many children - fleeing from war, hunger, poverty and social injustice. All too often, these brothers and sisters of ours meet along the way with death or, in any event, rejection by those who could offer them welcome and assistance.

On this glorious day, "let the earth rejoice, in shining splendour" (cf. Easter Proclamation), even though it is so often mistreated and greedily exploited, resulting in an alteration of natural equilibria. I think especially of those areas affected by climate change, which not infrequently causes drought or violent flooding, which then lead to food crises in different parts of the world.

Along with our brothers and sisters persecuted for their faith and their fidelity to the name of Christ, and before the evil that seems to have the upper hand in the life of so many people, let us hear once again the comforting words of the Lord: "Take courage; I have conquered the world!" (*Jn* 16:33) Today is the radiant day of this victory, for Christ has trampled death and destruction underfoot. By his Resurrection he has brought life and immortality to light (cf. *2 Tm* 1:10). "He has made us pass from enslavement to freedom, from sadness to joy, from mourning to jubilation, from darkness to light, from slavery to redemption. Therefore let us acclaim in his presence: Alleluia!" (Melito of Sardis, Easter Homily)

The Door of Salvation

To those in our society who have lost all hope and joy in life, to the elderly who struggle alone and feel their strength waning, to young people who seem to have no future, to all I once more address the words of the Risen One: "See, I am making all things new… To the thirsty I will give water as a gift from the spring of the water of life" (*Rv* 21:5-6). May this comforting message of Jesus help each of us to set out anew with greater courage and hope, to blaze trails of reconciliation with God and with all our brothers and sisters. How much we need this!

May there echo in your hearts, in your families and communities the announcement of the Resurrection, along with the warm light of the presence of the Living Jesus: a presence which brightens, comforts, forgives, gladdens. Jesus conquered evil at the root: he is the Door of Salvation, open wide so that each person may find mercy.

May you bring to all the joy and hope of the Risen Christ.[11]

EASTER MONDAY

On this Monday after Easter, called "Monday of the Angel" our hearts are again filled with the joy of Easter. After the Lenten season, the time of penance and conversion, which the Church has lived with particular intensity during this Holy Year of Mercy; after the striking celebrations of the Holy Triduum; today too, we stand before Jesus's empty tomb, and we meditate with wonder and gratitude on the Resurrection of the Lord.

Life has conquered death. Mercy and Love have conquered sin! We need faith and hope in order to open ourselves to this new and marvellous horizon. And we know that faith and hope are gifts from God, and we need to ask for them: "Lord, grant me faith, grant me hope! I need them so much!" Let us be permeated by the emotions that resound in the Easter sequence: "Yes, we are sure of it: Christ indeed from death is risen". The Lord has risen among us! This truth indelibly marked the lives of the Apostles who, after the Resurrection, again sensed the need to follow their Teacher and, having received the Holy Spirit, set out fearlessly to proclaim to all what they had seen with their own eyes and personally experienced.

The beginning of a new path

We are called to rediscover and to receive with particular intensity the comforting news of the Resurrection: "Christ my hope is arisen!" Since Christ is resurrected, we can look with new eyes and a new heart at every event of our lives, even the most negative ones. Moments of darkness, of failure and even sin can be transformed and announce the beginning of a new path. When we have reached the lowest point of our misery and our weakness, the Risen Christ gives us the strength to rise again. If we entrust ourselves to him, his grace saves us! The Lord, Crucified and Risen, is the full revelation of mercy, present and working throughout history. This is the Paschal message that resounds again today and will resound for the whole Easter Season until Pentecost.

The silent witness to the events of Jesus's Passion and Resurrection was Mary. She stood beside the cross: she did not fold in the face of pain; her faith made her strong. In the broken heart of the Mother, the flame of hope was kept ever burning. Let us ask her to help us too to fully accept the Easter proclamation of the Resurrection, so as to embody it in the concreteness of our daily lives.

May the Virgin Mary give us the faithful certitude that every step suffered on our journey, illuminated by the light of Easter, will become a blessing and a joy for us and for others, especially for those suffering because of selfishness and indifference.[12]

SECOND SUNDAY OF EASTER
(DIVINE MERCY SUNDAY)

"Jesus did many other signs in the presence of the disciples, which are not written in this book" (*Jn* 20:30). The Gospel is the book of God's mercy, to be read and reread, because everything that Jesus said and did is an expression of the Father's mercy. Not everything, however, was written down; the Gospel of mercy remains an open book, in which the signs of Christ's disciples - concrete acts of love and the best witness to mercy - continue to be written. We are all called to become living writers of the Gospel, heralds of the Good News to all men and women of today. We do this by practising the corporal and spiritual works of mercy, which are the hallmarks of the Christian life. By means of these simple yet powerful gestures, even when unseen, we can accompany the needy, bringing God's tenderness and consolation. Thus continues the great work of Jesus on Easter day, when he poured into the hearts of his fearful disciples the Father's mercy, bringing them the Holy Spirit who forgives sins and bestows joy.

Doors closed by sin

At the same time, the story we have just heard presents an evident contrast: there is the fear of the disciples, who gathered behind closed doors; and then there is the mission of Jesus, who sends them into the world to proclaim the message of forgiveness. This contrast may also be present in us, experienced as an interior struggle between a closed heart and the call of love to open doors closed by sin. It is a call that frees us to go out of ourselves. Christ, who for love entered through doors barred by sin, death and the powers of hell, wants to enter into each one of us to break open the locked doors of our hearts. Jesus, who by his Resurrection has overcome the fear and dread which imprison us, wishes to throw open our closed doors and send us out. The path that the Risen Master shows us is a one way street, it goes in only one direction: this means that we must move beyond ourselves to witness to the healing power of love that has conquered us. We see before us a humanity that is often wounded and fearful, a humanity that bears the scars of pain and uncertainty. Before the anguished cry for mercy and peace, we hear Jesus's inspiring invitation: "As the Father has sent me, even so I send you" (*Jn* 20:21).

In God's mercy, all of our infirmities find healing. His mercy, in fact, does not keep a distance: it seeks to encounter all forms of poverty and to free this world of so many types of slavery. Mercy desires to reach the wounds of all, to heal them. Being apostles of mercy means touching and soothing the wounds that today afflict the bodies and souls of many of our brothers and sisters. Curing these wounds, we profess Jesus, we make him present and alive; we allow others, who touch his mercy with their own hands, to recognise him as "Lord and God" (*Jn* 20:28), as did the Apostle Thomas. This is the mission that he entrusts to us. So many people ask to be listened to and to be understood. The Gospel of mercy, to be proclaimed and written in our daily lives, seeks people with patient and open hearts, "good Samaritans" who understand compassion and silence before the mystery of each brother and sister. The Gospel of mercy requires generous and joyful servants, people who love freely without expecting anything in return.

This peace is born ever anew

"Peace be with you!" (*Jn* 20:21) is the greeting of Jesus to his disciples; this same peace awaits men and women of our own day. It is not a negotiated peace, it is not the absence of conflict: it is his peace, the peace that comes from the heart of the Risen Lord, the peace that has defeated sin, fear and death. It is a peace that does not divide but unites; it is a peace that does not abandon us but makes us feel listened to and loved; it is a peace that persists even in pain and enables hope to blossom. This peace, as on the day of Easter, is born ever anew by the forgiveness of God which calms our anxious hearts. To be bearers of his peace: this is the mission entrusted to the Church on Easter day. In Christ, we are born to be instruments of reconciliation, to bring the Father's forgiveness to everyone, to reveal his loving face through concrete gestures of mercy.

In the responsorial Psalm we heard these words: "His love endures forever" (*Ps* 117/118:2). Truly, God's mercy is forever; it never ends, it never runs out, it never gives up when faced with closed doors, and it never tires. In this forever we find strength in moments of trial and weakness because we are sure that God does not abandon us. He remains with us forever. Let us give thanks for so great a love, which we find impossible to grasp; it is immense! Let us pray for the grace to never grow tired of drawing from the well of the Father's mercy and bringing it to the world. Let us ask that we too may be merciful, to spread the power of the Gospel everywhere, and to write those pages of the Gospel which John the Apostle did not write.[13]

THIRD SUNDAY OF EASTER

Today's Gospel recounts the third apparition of the Risen Jesus to the disciples, with the account of the miraculous catch on the shore of the lake of Galilee (cf. *Jn* 21:1-19). The narrative is situated in the context of the everyday life of the disciples, who returned to their land and to their work as fishermen, after the shocking days of the Passion, death and Resurrection of the Lord. It was difficult for them to understand what had taken place. Even though everything seemed finished, Jesus "seeks" his disciples once more. It is he who goes to seek them. This time he meets them at the lake, where they have spent the night in their boats catching nothing. The nets appear empty, in a certain sense, like the tally of their experience with Jesus: they met him, they left everything to follow him, full of hope... and now? Yes, they saw he was risen, but then they thought: "He went away and left us... It was like a dream...".

So it is that at sunrise Jesus presents himself on the lakeshore; however they do not recognise him (cf. v. 4). The Lord says to those tired and disappointed fishermen: "Cast the net on the right side of the boat, and you will find some" (v. 6). The disciples trust in Jesus and the result is an incredibly abundant catch. At this point John turns to Peter and says: "It is the Lord!" (v. 7) Right away Peter throws himself into the water and swims to the shore, toward Jesus. In that exclamation, "It is the Lord!" there is all the enthusiasm of the Paschal faith, full of joy and wonder, which sharply contrasts with the disappearance, the dejection, the sense of powerlessness that had accumulated in the disciples' hearts. The presence of the Risen Jesus transforms everything: darkness has become light, futile work has again become fruitful and promising, the sense of weariness and abandonment give way to a new impetus and to the certainty that he is with us.

Invincible hope

From that time, these same sentiments enliven the Church, the Community of the Risen One. All of us are the community of the Risen One! At first glance it might sometimes seem that the darkness of evil and the toil of daily living have got the upper hand, the Church knows with certainty that the now everlasting light of Easter shines upon those who follow the Lord Jesus. The great message of the Resurrection instils in the hearts of believers profound joy and invincible hope. Christ is truly risen! Today too, the Church continues to make this joyous message resound: joy and hope continue to flow in hearts, in faces, in gestures, in words. We Christians are all called to communicate this message of resurrection to those we meet, especially to those who suffer, to those who are alone, to those who find themselves in precarious conditions, to the sick, to refugees, to the marginalised. Let us make a ray of the light of the Risen Christ, a sign of his powerful mercy, reach everyone.

May he, the Lord, also renew in us the Paschal faith. May he render us ever more aware of our mission at the service of the Gospel and of our brothers and sisters; may he fill us with his Holy Spirit so that, sustained by the intercession of Mary, with all the Church we may proclaim the greatness of his love and the abundance of his mercy.[14]

Fourth Sunday of Easter

Today's Gospel (*Jn* 10:27-30) offers us some of Jesus's expressions during the feast of the dedication of the Temple of Jerusalem, which is celebrated at the end of December. He is found on the Temple grounds, and perhaps that enclosed sacred space suggested to him the image of the sheepfold and the shepherd. Jesus is presented as "the Good Shepherd", and says, "My sheep hear my voice, and I know them, and they follow me; and I give them eternal life, and they shall never perish, and no one shall snatch them out of my hand" (vv. 27-28). These words help us to understand that no one can call himself a follower of Jesus, if he does not listen to his voice. And this "listening" should not be understood in a superficial way, but in an engaging way, to the point of making possible a true mutual understanding, from which one can come to a generous following, expressed in the words, "and they follow me" (v. 27). It is a matter of listening not only with ears, but listening with the heart!

And so, the image of the shepherd and the sheep indicates the close relationship that Jesus wants to establish with each one of us. He is our guide, our teacher, our friend, our model, but above all he is our Saviour. In fact, the following expressions from the Gospel passage affirm, "I give them eternal life, and they shall never perish, and no one shall snatch them out of my hand" (v. 28). Who can say that? Only Jesus, because the "hand" of Jesus is one thing with the "hand" of the Father, and the Father is "greater than all" (cf. v. 29).

Secure in the hands of Jesus

These words communicate to us a sense of absolute security and immense tenderness. Our life is fully secure in the hands of Jesus and the Father, which are a single thing: a unique love, a unique mercy, revealed once and for all in the sacrifice of the cross. To save the lost sheep which we all are, the Shepherd became lamb, and let himself be immolated so as to take upon himself and to take away the sin of the world. In this way he has given us life, life in abundance (cf. *Jn* 10:10). This mystery is renewed, in an always surprising humility, on the Eucharistic table. It is there that the sheep gather to nourish themselves; it is there that they become one, among themselves and with the Good Shepherd.

Because of this we are no longer afraid: our life is now saved from perdition. Nothing and no one can take us from the hands of Jesus, because nothing and no one can overcome his love. Jesus's love is invincible. The evil one, the great enemy of God and of his creatures, attempts in many ways to take eternal life from us. But the evil one can do nothing if we ourselves do not open the doors of our hearts to him, by following his deceitful enticements.

The Virgin Mary heard and obediently followed the voice of the Good Shepherd. May she help us to welcome with joy Jesus's invitation to become his disciples, and to always live in the certainty of being in the paternal hands of the Father.[15]

Fifth Sunday of Easter

"By this everyone will know that you are my disciples, if you have love for one another" (*Jn* 13:35).

What an enormous responsibility the Lord gives us today! He tells us that the world will recognise the disciples of Jesus by the way they love one another. Love, in other words, is the Christian's identity card, the only valid "document" identifying us as Christians. It is the only valid document. If this card expires and is not constantly renewed, we stop being witnesses of the Master. So I ask you: Do you wish to say yes to Jesus's invitation to be his disciples? Do you wish to be his faithful friends? The true friends of Jesus stand out essentially by the *genuine love*; not some "pie in the sky" love; no, it is a genuine love that shines forth in their way of life. Love is always shown in real actions. Those who are not real and genuine and who speak of love are like characters is a soap opera, some fake love story. Do you want to experience his love? Do you want this love: yes or no? Let us learn from him, for his words are a *school of life*, a school where we learn to love. This is a task which we must engage in every day: to learn how to love.

Before all else, love *is beautiful*, it is the path to happiness. But it is not an easy path. It is demanding and it requires effort. Think, for example, of when we receive a gift. It makes us happy, but receiving a gift means that someone generous has invested time and effort; by their gift they also give us a bit of themselves, a sacrifice they have made. Think too of the gift that your parents and group leaders have given you in allowing you to come to Rome for this Jubilee day dedicated to you. They planned, organised, and prepared everything for you, and this made them happy, even if it meant that they had to give up a trip for themselves. This is putting love into action. To love *means to give*, not only something material, but also something of one's self: one's own time, one's friendship, one's own abilities.

Love is a free gift

Love is a *free gift* which calls for an open heart; love is a responsibility, but *a noble responsibility* which is life-long; it is *a daily task* for those who can achieve great dreams! Woe to your people who do not know how to dream, who do not dare to dream! If a person of your age is not able to dream, if they have already gone into retirement… this is not good. Love is nurtured by trust, respect and forgiveness. Love does not happen because we talk about it, but when we live it: it is not a sweet poem to study and memorise, but is a life choice to put into practice! How can we grow in love? The secret, once again, is the Lord: Jesus gives us himself in the Mass, he offers us forgives and peace in Confession. There we learn to receive his love, to make it ours and to give it to the world. And when loving seems hard, when it is difficult to say no to something wrong, look up at Jesus on the cross, embrace the cross and don't ever let go of his hand. He will point you ever higher, and pick you up whenever you fall. Throughout life we will fall many times, because we are sinners, we are weak. But there is always the hand of God who picks us up, who raises us up. Jesus wants us to be up on our feet! Think of the beautiful word Jesus said to the paralytic: "Arise!" God has created us to be on our feet. There is a lovely song that mountain climbers sing as they climb. It goes like this: "In climbing, the important thing is not to not fall, but to not remain fallen!". To have the courage to pick oneself up, to allow oneself to be raised up by Jesus. And his hand is often given through the hand of a friend, through the hand of one's parents, through the hand of those who accompany us throughout life. Jesus himself is present in them. So arise! God wants us up on our feet, ever on our feet!

I know that you are capable of acts of great friendship and goodness. With these you are called to build the future, *together* with others and for others, but never *against* anyone! One never builds "against"; this is called "destruction". You will do amazing things if you prepare well, starting now, by living your youth and all its gifts to the fullest and without fear of hard work. Be like sporting champions, who attain high goals by quiet daily effort and practice. Let your daily programme be the works of mercy. Enthusiastically practise them, so as to be *champions in life*, *champions in love!* In this way you will be recognised as disciples of Jesus. In this way, you will have the identification card of the Christian. And I promise you: your joy *will* be complete.[16]

Sixth Sunday of Easter

Today's Gospel takes us back to the Upper Room. During the Last Supper, before confronting his Passion and death on the cross, Jesus promises the Apostles the gift of the Holy Spirit, who will have the task of teaching and recalling [Jesus's] words to the community of disciples. Jesus says: "the Counsellor, the Holy Spirit, whom the Father will send in my name, he will teach you all things, and bring to your remembrance all that I have said to you" (*Jn* 14:26). Teach and recall. This is what the Holy Spirit does in our hearts.

At the moment in which he is about to return to the Father, Jesus foretells of the coming of the Spirit who will first teach the disciples to understand the Gospel ever more fully, in order to welcome it in their existence and to render it living and operative by their witness. While he is about to entrust to the Apostles - which in fact means "envoys" - the mission of taking the Gospel to all the world, Jesus promises that they will not be alone. The Holy Spirit, the Counsellor, will be with them, and will be beside them, moreover, will be within them, to protect and support them. Jesus returns to the Father but continues to accompany and teach his disciples through the gift of the Holy Spirit.

The second aspect of the Holy Spirit's mission consists in helping the Apostles to remember Jesus's words. The Spirit has the task of reawakening the memory, recalling Jesus's words. The divine Teacher has already communicated all that he intended to entrust to the Apostles: with Him, the Word made flesh, the revelation is complete. The Spirit will recall Jesus's teachings in the various concrete circumstances of life, so that they may be put into practice. That is precisely what still happens today in the Church, guided by the light and the power of the Holy Spirit, so that he may bring to everyone the gift of salvation, which is the love and mercy of God. For example, each day when you read - as I have advised you - a passage, a passage of the Gospel, ask the Holy Spirit: "Let me understand and remember these words of Jesus". Then read the passage, every day... But first the prayer to the Spirit, who is in our heart: "Let me remember and understand".

We are not alone

We are not alone: Jesus is close to us, among us, within us! His new presence in history happens through the gift of the Holy Spirit, through whom it is possible to instil a living relationship with him, the Crucified and Risen One. The Spirit, flowing within us through the Sacraments of Baptism and Confirmation, acts in our life. He guides us in the way to think, to act, to distinguish between what is good and what is bad; he helps us to practise the charity of Jesus, his giving of himself to others, especially to the most needy. We are not alone! The sign of the presence of the Holy Spirit is also the peace that Jesus gives to his disciples: "My peace I give to you" (v. 27). It is different from what mankind hopes for or tries to achieve. The peace of Jesus flows from victory over sin, over selfishness which impedes us from loving one another as brothers and sisters. It is a gift of God and a sign of his presence. Each disciple called today to follow Jesus carrying the cross, receives within him or herself the peace of the Crucified and Risen One in the certainty of his victory and in expectation of his definitive coming.

May the Virgin Mary help us to welcome with docility the Holy Spirit as interior Teacher and as the living Memory of Christ on the daily journey.[17]

SEVENTH SUNDAY OF EASTER (ASCENSION)

Today, we are celebrating the Ascension of Jesus into Heaven, which occurred forty days after Easter. Let us contemplate the mystery of Jesus who leaves our earthly space to enter the fullness of the glory of God, taking our humanity with him. In other words, our humanity enters heaven for the first time. The Gospel of Luke describes the reaction of the disciples before the Lord who "parted from them and was carried up into heaven" (24:51). They had no sorrow nor dismay, but "they worshiped him, and returned to Jerusalem with great joy" (v. 52). It was the return of those who no longer feared the city that had rejected the Master, who had seen Judas's betrayal and Peter's denial; who had seen the dispersion of the disciples and the brutality of a power that felt threatened. Since that day, the Apostles and every disciple of Christ have been able to live in Jerusalem and in all cities of the world, even in those most afflicted by injustice and violence, because above every city there is the same heaven and every inhabitant can lift his or her gaze with hope. Jesus, God, is true man, with his human body, he is in heaven! This is our hope, it is still ours, and we are firm in this hope if we look to heaven.

In this heaven lives that God who revealed himself so closely as to take on the face of a man, Jesus of Nazareth. He remains for us always the God-with-us - let us remember this: Emmanuel, God with us - and he never leaves us alone! We can look to heaven in order to recognise our future before us. In the Ascension of Jesus, Crucified and Risen, there is the promise of our participation in the fullness of life with God.

Bear this witness

Before departing from his friends, Jesus, referring to the event of his death and Resurrection, said to them: "You are witnesses of these things" (v. 48). In other words the disciples, the Apostles, were witnesses of the death and Resurrection of Christ, on that day, also of the Ascension of Christ. In fact, after seeing their Lord ascend into heaven, the disciples returned to the city as witnesses joyfully proclaiming to all the new life which comes from the Crucified and Risen One, in whose name "repentance and forgiveness of sins should be preached to all nations" (cf. v. 47). This is the witness - born not only with words but with everyday life - the witness that every Sunday should flow from our churches so as to enter during the week into homes, offices, schools, meeting and recreational places, hospitals, prisons, homes for the elderly, in places crowded with immigrants, in the peripheries of the city... We must bear this witness every week: Christ is with us: Jesus rose to heaven, he is with us: Christ lives!

Jesus assured us that in this proclamation and in this witness we shall be "clothed with power from on high" (v. 49), that is, with the power of the Holy Spirit. Here is the secret to this mission: the presence among us of the Risen Lord, who with the gift of the Holy Spirit, continues to open our minds and our hearts, to proclaim his love and his mercy even in the most resistant areas of our cities. The Holy Spirit is the true artisan of the multiform witness that the Church and every baptised person renders in the world. Therefore, we must never neglect to meditate in prayer in order to praise God and invoke the gift of the Holy Spirit. This week, which leads us to the feast of Pentecost, let us remain spiritually in the Upper Room, together with the Virgin Mary, to receive the Holy Spirit. Let us do so now too, in communion with the faithful gathered in the Shrine of Pompeii for the traditional Supplication.[18]

Pentecost

Today we celebrate the great feast of Pentecost, which completes the season of Easter, fifty days after the Resurrection of Christ. The liturgy invites us to open our mind and our heart to the gift of the Holy Spirit, whom Jesus promised on several occasions to his disciples: the first and most important gift that he obtained for us with his Resurrection. Jesus himself asked the Father for this gift, as today's Gospel Reading attests, during the Last Supper. Jesus says to his disciples: "If you love me, you will keep my commandments. And I will pray the Father, and he will give you another Counsellor, to be with you for ever" (*Jn* 14:15-16).

These words remind us first of all that love for a person, and for the Lord, is shown not with words but with deeds; and also, "observing the commandments" should be understood in the existential sense, so as to embrace the whole of life. In fact, being Christian does not mean mainly belonging to a certain culture or adhering to a certain doctrine, but rather joining one's own life, in all its aspects, to the person of Jesus and, through him, to the Father. For this purpose Jesus promises the outpouring of the Holy Spirit to his disciples. Owing to the Holy Spirit, to the Love that unites the Father and the Son and proceeds from them, we may all live the very life of Jesus. The Spirit, in fact, teaches us all things, that is, the single indispensable thing: to love as God loves.

Deeply inspired by the Holy Spirit

In promising the Holy Spirit, Jesus defines him as "another Counsellor" (v. 16), which means Paraclete, Advocate, Intercessor, in other words, the One who helps us, protects us, is at our side on the journey of life and in the struggle for good and that against evil. Jesus says "another Counsellor" because he is the first, he himself, who became flesh precisely to take our human condition upon himself and free it from the slavery of sin.

Moreover, the Holy Spirit plays a role in teaching and remembrance. Teaching and remembrance. Jesus told us: "the Counsellor, the Holy Spirit, whom the Father will send in my name, he will teach you all things, and bring to your remembrance all that I have said to you" (v. 26). The Holy Spirit does not bring a different teaching, but renders alive and brings into effect the teaching of Jesus, so that the passage of time may neither erase nor diminish it. The Holy Spirit instils this teaching in our heart, helps us to internalise it, making it become a part of us, flesh of our flesh. At the same time, he prepares our heart to be truly capable of receiving the words and example of the Lord. Every time the word of Jesus is received with joy in our heart, this is the work of the Holy Spirit.

Let us pray the Regina Caeli together - for the last time this year - invoking the maternal intercession of the Virgin Mary. May she obtain for us the grace to be deeply inspired by the Holy Spirit, to witness with evangelical simplicity to Christ, opening ourselves ever more fully to his love.[19]

Endnotes

[1] Homily, Holy Mass, blessing and imposition of the ashes, Ash Wednesday, 10th February 2016.

[2] Homily, First Sunday of Lent, 14th February 2016.

[3] Homily, Second Sunday of Lent, 21st February 2016.

[4] Angelus, Third Sunday of Lent, 28th February 2016.

[5] Angelus, Fourth Sunday of Lent, 6th March 2016.

[6] Angelus, Fifth Sunday of Lent, 13th March 2016.

[7] Homily, Celebration of Palm Sunday of The Passion Of The Lord, Sunday, 20th March 2016.

[8] General Audience, Wednesday, 23rd March 2016.

[9] Homily of His Holiness Pope Francis, C.A.R.A. Auxilium, Castelnuovo di Porto (Rome), Holy Thursday, 24th March 2016.

[10] Homily, Paschal Vigil, Holy Saturday, 26th March 2016.

[11] Urbi Et Orbi Message for Easter 2016, Sunday, 27th March 2016.

[12] Regina Cæli, Easter Monday, 28th March 2016.

[13] Homily, Second Sunday of Easter, 3rd April 2016.

[14] Regina Cæli, Third Sunday of Easter, 10th April 2016.

[15] Regina Caeli, Fourth Sunday of Easter, 17th April 2016.

[16] Homily, Fifth Sunday of Easter, 24th April 2016.

[17] Regina Cæli, Sixth Sunday of Easter, 1st May 2016.

[18] Regina Cæli, Seventh Sunday of Easter (Ascension), 8th May 2016.

[19] Regina Cæli, Solemnity of Pentecost, Sunday, 15th May 2016.

Has this book helped you?
Spread the word!

@CTSpublishers

/CTSpublishers

ctscatholiccompass.org

Let us know!
marketing@ctsbooks.org
+44 (0)207 640 0042

Learn, love, live your faith.
www.CTSbooks.org